Create and Curate

500 Ideas for Artists & Writers

Create and Curate

Published by Unleash Press
© 2023 by Jen Knox and Ashley Holloway
Notable Contributor: Sascha Ealey
Book cover design by Christopher Shanahan
All rights reserved.
No part of this publication may be reproduced, distributed, or transmitted in any form or by any means, including photocopying, recording, or other electronic or mechanical methods, without the prior written permission of the publisher, except in the case of brief quotations embodied in critical reviews and specific other noncommercial uses permitted by copyright law.
Printed in the United States of America
ISBN 9781737519454

500 Ideas for Artists & Writers

Contents

Introduction

Curate

Create

Reflect

Connect

Alchemize

On Inspiration
(from the Unleash team)

Create and Curate

500 Ideas for Artists & Writers

Introduction

Welcome to this tiny, handy book of 500 creative prompts by the Unleash team that offers inspiration to artists, writers, or anyone who would like to live more creatively. It is our belief that all the seemingly ordinary details and nuances of our lives are opportunities to explore imagination through a variety of mediums. We also believe that creativity is good for the mind, body, and spirit.

We put this book together as a fun way to explore different approaches to sharing stories and emotional truths through simple (and sometimes silly) prompts. If you are just beginning your creative journey or reestablishing a creative practice, you might be surprised how a little prompt can open up worlds. If you're an established writer or artist, you can use this book to hone your craft or get back to the joy of pure creative expression.

Create and Curate

Our challenge to you, my friend, is to aim to respond to as many prompts as you can in the next thirty days. Then see if you can top that number the next month. One prompt each week is a good place to start, but you might get up to a prompt a day. You can go systematically, keeping to themes, or jump around and cross the prompts off as you go.

Remember, artistic expression is like a passport that can take you around the world and beyond without the bother of having to step foot in an airport, remove your shoes, and lift your arms for transportation security officers (see the *Reflect* section for an airport prompt). Go curate, create, reflect, connect, and alchemize. And remember to have fun! We look forward to hearing how it goes.

–The Unleash Team

500 Ideas for Artists & Writers

Key

A = Art prompts

W = Writing prompts

Note: Bonus points for breaking all the rules.

500 Ideas for Artists & Writers

CURATE

Create and Curate

- [ ] Create a typical ad with a not-so-typical product.

- [ ] Make a piece based on your favorite word.

- [ ] Research as much as you can about your favorite flower. Illustrate its ideal environment.

- [ ] Design a tattoo based on your favorite song.

- [ ] Depict your favorite story as an image.

- [ ] Everyday things with secret uses.

- [ ] Mirror and light … go!

- [ ] Spring cleaning can mean more than cleaning the house. Create a work that speaks to a cleared space.

500 Ideas for Artists & Writers

- ☐ Go for a walk around your neighborhood. Take photographs of ten random objects on your walk. Create a story or work of art that combines these ten objects.

- ☐ Create a visual depiction of your bucket list.

- ☐ Depict your inner critic as the person/monster/cartoon it is.

- ☐ Depict the sky before and after the storm. Side by side.

- ☐ The view she has, and the view she wishes she had.

- ☐ Use old food cartons or boxes to create a collage.

- ☐ Create a comical portrait of your pet (if you don't have a pet, a neighbor's or friend's pet will do).

- ☐ Depict your favorite toy when you were a kid.

Create and Curate

- ☐ Take a ride on public transit. Develop an image around one of the passengers. Who are they? Where are they going? Where are they coming from?

- ☐ What would your child self think about your life now? Draw or paint the answer.

- ☐ Think of a color. Now go for a walk (however long you would like) and make note of all the things you see that are that color. When you return, create a piece of art based on these things.

- ☐ Create a piece of art based on your alter-ego.

- ☐ The Grim Reaper puts you in charge to take a much-needed vacation. Take the work from here.

- ☐ Create a piece of art that depicts the energy of summer.

- ☐ A scene at a community pool.

500 Ideas for Artists & Writers

- ☐ Draw your ideal world as you saw it as a young child.

- ☐ High school cafeterias.

- ☐ The well-intentioned young person who breaks bad, and the reflective adult they become.

- ☐ Bus stops and magic.

- ☐ Everyone under 13 and over 18 disappears.

- ☐ Finding true love for the first time after retirement.

- ☐ Traveling out of the country and falling in love with a new location.

- ☐ Retirement home shenanigans.

- ☐ Create a piece using only one color in different shades and textures.

Create and Curate

- ☐ Reinterpret an image from a travel photograph.

- ☐ Draw the hands of the person you'll one day become.

- ☐ The luggage is lined up by the front door. Depict the scene.

- ☐ Create your own nutrition label (either realistic or absurd).

- ☐ Tell your life story in a collage.

- ☐ Depict your profession in an abstract way.

- ☐ Use the natural elements to inspire a work of art.

- ☐ Design a piece of jewelry.

- ☐ Choreograph a dance to your favorite jingle.

- ☐ Use a favorite quote to inspire a piece.

500 Ideas for Artists & Writers

- ☐ Close your eyes and draw the room you are in.

- ☐ Design the ideal outfit.

- ☐ Imagine that your favorite stuffed animal as a child had a home. What would it look like?

- ☐ Depict your favorite holiday in an image.

- ☐ Take a boring piece of furniture in your house and find a way to make it brilliant.

- ☐ Think about a ritual or routine that brings you peace. Show it in a piece of art.

- ☐ Make a playlist for artists (share it with us, please).

- ☐ Create a piece of art based on the last dream you remember.

Create and Curate

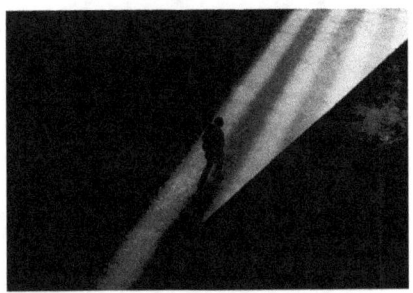

W

- ☐ Write a story from the perspective of your (or someone else's) shadow.

- ☐ Your character meets and overcomes their greatest fear.

- ☐ Set a timer for one minute. Write as much as you can.

- ☐ Write a short story about this day 100 years in the past.

500 Ideas for Artists & Writers

- [ ] Use your daily horoscope as the basis for a story.

- [ ] What part of childhood did you never want to let go of but eventually had to leave behind?

- [ ] Write about bangs.

- [ ] A holiday spent with every single one of your family members in one location.

- [ ] Read job reviews of various workers in your industry and write a short story from the perspective of an employee of a similar fictional company.

- [ ] Write directions on how to do something, such as making a paper airplane, a cake, or repotting a plant.

- [ ] Write a fictional story about jury duty.

- [ ] The concert began peacefully.

- [ ] Your favorite winter food.

Create and Curate

- [ ] A Zoom meeting goes wrong.

- [ ] An everyday household location turns out to be a time machine.

- [ ] The luxury car that is parked in front of a dollar store ... who does this belong to?

- [ ] Think about your childhood home in a different dimension. The basement sound turns out to be more than just the water heater. What is it?

- [ ] Write about a house cat's day in the wild.

- [ ] A person frequents a bridge that overlooks a freeway.

- [ ] An abandoned mall is purchased by a millionaire with questionable intentions.

- [ ] The public transport system in your city at 4 a.m. on a Tuesday.

- [ ] A shared ride that went wrong.

500 Ideas for Artists & Writers

- ☐ Write about being lost in an unfamiliar place.

- ☐ Write a story using a single emotion as the central character. Use first-person narrative.

- ☐ Imagine you meet your doppelganger and a strange attraction develops.

- ☐ Being trapped in an elevator.

- ☐ A cooking contest is being broadcast live when one of the judges is poisoned after tasting one of the contestants' dishes.

- ☐ Write 5 adjectives that describe each of your senses (taste, sight, touch, hear and smell).

- ☐ Write a poem about your morning routine.

- ☐ Christmas becomes the scariest time of year. Write the backstory of how and why this happened.

- ☐ You receive an item in the mail without a return address that contains an item you didn't realize you had lost.

Create and Curate

- [ ] Write a story inspired by the fashion of the 1970s, 1980s, or 1990s (or all three).

- [ ] Write a story from the perspective of Father Time.

- [ ] Attend a concert or stage performance. Write a story about what is going on behind the curtains.

- [ ] Write a story about taxidermy.

- [ ] Write about a daily ritual that goes wrong.

- [ ] Grocery shopping then and now.

- [ ] Grocery shopping now and in the future.

- [ ] Your favorite kid's book comes to life.

- [ ] Write about an unexpected experience in a parking lot or parking garage.

- [ ] Write the dialogue that would occur if you met Einstein at a Starbucks.

500 Ideas for Artists & Writers

- [ ] What was your favorite show when you were a kid? Write a story with you as the protagonist of this show.

- [ ] A text or email you didn't mean to send.

- [ ] What might happen if your walls began to melt?

- [ ] What would the world look like with no internet for fourteen days?

- [ ] What story would your pet(s) tell if they could speak?

- [ ] It's Friday the 13th ... write about what happens on this day.

- [ ] Set a fantastical story in an ordinary location you visit every day.

Create and Curate

CREATE

500 Ideas for Artists & Writers

A

- [ ] Someone is living in the dollhouse. Draw! Paint!

- [ ] What is on the other side of the trap door?

- [ ] Use a recent dream as inspiration for an image.

- [ ] Go to a museum or gallery (virtual or in-person), pick a piece of artwork, and write or draw for twenty minutes straight. See what happens.

- [ ] Open your favorite book to a random page and pick a sentence. Write it down and then keep going, see where it takes you. In the end, delete the original sentence (no one wants to get sued).

- [ ] It snowed 10 inches in July. In New York City.

Create and Curate

- ☐ Describe something intangible, such as laughter or emotion.

- ☐ When they got married, everyone thought it was a mistake.

- ☐ What it feels like to pay off a loan or get a loan for the first time.

- ☐ Write a story or create a piece of art based on your favorite song.

- ☐ Go to a museum or gallery (virtual or in-person) and write what life might be like from the perspective of the security guard, only the security guard isn't who they seem to be.

- ☐ What happened to the superhero after retirement?

- ☐ Write a story from the perspective of the Mona Lisa looking out at the crowds.

- ☐ Visit a hardware store that sells paint. Use a color palette that catches your eye as

500 Ideas for Artists & Writers

inspiration for a story. Try to choose a palette you wouldn't normally choose.

- [ ] A private helicopter shows up at the talent show.

- [ ] A private bunker is no longer private.

- [ ] What is Rodin's *The Thinker* thinking about?

- [ ] Take the first sentence from one book, and the last sentence from a different book. Combine them to create a story (delete the two original sentences).

- [ ] Choose the setting of your favorite novel. Write a tourist guide based on that place.

- [ ] Use the internet to access a virtual tour of an art gallery or museum. Spend some time "strolling." Find an object that appeals to you and imagine how you might describe the object or piece of art to someone who is visually impaired.

Create and Curate

- [ ] Have someone you know draw a random squiggle on a blank piece of paper. Use the shape to create a drawing. Experiment with different shapes, colors, and mediums.

- [ ] Grab a pencil and some blank paper. Start writing whatever words come to mind, but don't let your pencil leave the page. Use the entire page and don't worry about uniformity or overlapping lines. Keep writing to see what becomes of it.

- [ ] Using magazines or newspaper flyers, cut out images and arrange the pieces by color tone. Glue the pieces to a canvas to create an image.

- [ ] Recreate a work of art you admire. Recreate it two more times, only with less and less detail, making it more abstract each time.

- [ ] Cut images from magazines, newspapers, and scrap paper to create a self-portrait collage. Use as little color or as much color as you would like.

500 Ideas for Artists & Writers

- ☐ Fingerpaint.

- ☐ Create a piece of art using only letters and numbers.

- ☐ Create art that depicts the grind of middle age.

- ☐ An atheist marries an evangelist.

- ☐ Play with your food.

- ☐ Play with your food wrappers.

- ☐ Imagine a newly discovered animal and depict it in a drawing or painting.

- ☐ Draw a favorite scent.

- ☐ Depict a coffee shop on Mars.

- ☐ An upside-down world.

- ☐ Create your own Halloween costume from things around the house.

Create and Curate

- [ ] A confrontation begins in the hallway just before the last bell. Show the aftermath.

- [ ] Create a Halloween costume for a pet that doesn't exist.

- [ ] Make a portrait of one of your friends' pets, and truly work to capture the pet's essence using only primary colors.

- [ ] Next time you clean your house, do everything you can to make it a celebratory experience (think loud music, dancing, cake).

- [ ] Imagine a time in the future when farming does not exist any longer. What does the world look like?

- [ ] Depict a laboratory that has been shut down for questionable practices.

- [ ] Explore the phenomenon, mystery, and beauty of twins in an image.

- [ ] The ship in the bottle disappeared. What's there now?

500 Ideas for Artists & Writers

- [ ] If you can find one, walk a labyrinth, then, from memory, draw one.

- [ ] We followed a set of footprints. Show where they led.

- [ ] Make a vision board for a robot with big dreams.

- [ ] Come up with a new fad or trend—go big!

- [ ] Find 5-6 kind or encouraging letters, cards, or emails you've received, print them out, respectively, and make them into a collage to frame.

- [ ] Make a sculpture out of old electronic devices.

Create and Curate

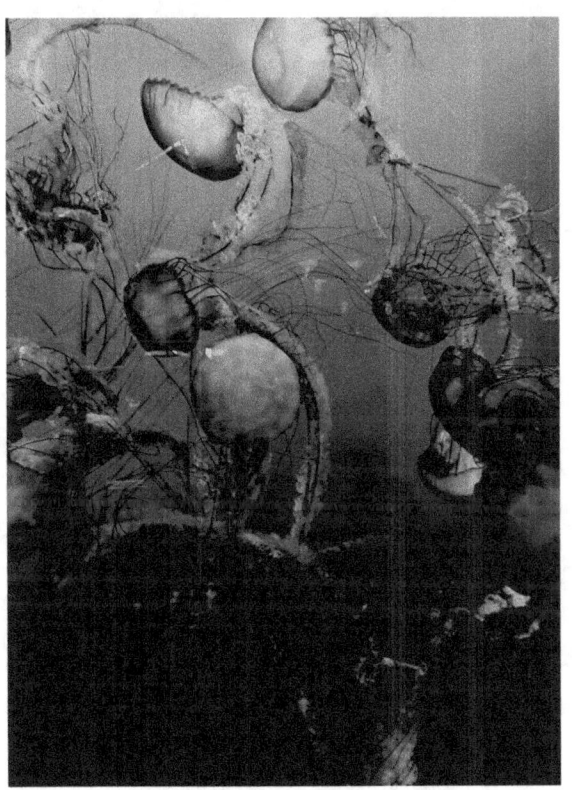

500 Ideas for Artists & Writers

W

- "I quit." Begin a story with a person leaving a long-time career.

- "No one ever told me…" Begin a story with this line. When you run out of things to say, begin again with the same phrase. Repeat a third time.

- The equinox was supposed to be about balance, but when the bonfire took over, everything changed.

- Everyone came to him for advice due to his motivational sermons, but his life was falling apart.

- The guru told her to go on a journey. She never expected to end up where she did.

- Who needs a horoscope? The planets told her what to do.

Create and Curate

- [ ] Who knew you could make so much money preaching on YouTube?

- [ ] A male mail-order bride.

- [ ] Imagine you are an Uber driver and you have just picked up Dolly Parton as a passenger. Write the dialogue of how the scene might play out.

- [ ] Using the language style of Shakespearean times, write out how one might place an order for a pizza by telephone (and if you are gutsy enough… order it!).

- [ ] Write a story 100 years in the future. Your character is reading the news.

- [ ] The Tarot reading foretold it all.

- [ ] "Don't go in there!" Write a story about protected spaces.

- [ ] "I was trying to protect you." Write a story about a character whose lie-by-omission is revealed.

500 Ideas for Artists & Writers

- [ ] What happens when superheroes retire?

- [ ] "Most adventure stories don't start with asking people to sign an insurance waiver." Write a story about a grand adventure.

- [ ] "Who would you like to speak to?" the medium asked. Write a story in which a psychic medium channels someone for your character, but the message that comes through is unexpected.

- [ ] "The genie warned him that was a bad idea for a third wish." Begin a story about finding a genie in a bottle.

- [ ] "We will protect the people at every turn..." Write a story about a young politician who finds out how difficult it is to lead.

- [ ] "We never understood why the family never left the house." Write a story in the first-person plural (we) about a neighborhood family that is mysterious. You can reveal the mystery at the end or leave it open.

Create and Curate

- "Grandma locked us in the bathroom again."

- "How could you!" Begin a story about an argument.

- "I felt as though I was moving in slow motion." Write a story about a chase.

- "I don't think that is the right button," someone said, just as I pressed the button… Begin a story where you made a grave error.

- "And that's the day when I met my mother for the first time." Write a story about displacement.

- "Suddenly, the Ferris wheel started turning faster and faster…" Write a story that takes place at a carnival.

- "I knew that smell; you can never forget the stench of death." Use only dialogue to depict the scene.

500 Ideas for Artists & Writers

- ☐ "That was the moment I realized I could breathe underwater." Write a story about a new-found skill.

- ☐ "I hadn't noticed that door before. It was almost as if it suddenly appeared out of nowhere." Write a story about a journey.

- ☐ "I cracked the egg into the frying pan but it wasn't an egg after all." Write a story about an unexpected find.

- ☐ "Guard this with your life," he said, as he stuffed the burlap bag in my hands and fled into the night.

- ☐ Find an entertaining classified advertisement (looking for love, looking to buy microwave, looking to sell a collection of wigs), and begin to write a scene.

- ☐ Write a story or create art based on the Wikipedia subject of the day.

- ☐ Write a story or create art incorporating the Thesaurus.com word of the day.

Create and Curate

- [ ] Write about a person who clicks every pop-up.

- [ ] Write about a mastermind hacker who is not motivated by money.

- [ ] Write about a person who lives off the grid for a year.

- [ ] Singularity: write or depict a scene in which a person merges with the internet.

- [ ] Write a story using a search engine (Google, Edge) as the main character.

- [ ] Write a story about a specific font.

- [ ] Technology today is such that human memories can be extracted from DNA.

- [ ] Write about what would happen if the past and the future co-exist.

- [ ] You lose the ability to distinguish between reality from illusion. Write what happens next.

500 Ideas for Artists & Writers

- ☐ Write an obituary for Satan.

- ☐ Write about a cuckoo clock that cannot keep the proper time.

- ☐ Write about the child of a professional clown.

- ☐ The new app seemed fun at first, but it soon became dangerous.

- ☐ "She got kicked out of hospice."

- ☐ Write about a fictional world run by children.

- ☐ When grocery shopping, choose a product and see if you can write an advertisement for it in fifty words or less.

Create and Curate

REFLECT

500 Ideas for Artists & Writers

- [ ] Use an old, cherished family recipe as the basis for art.

- [ ] Reflect on some of the most memorable conversations you've had. Use the best line or two that inspire a work of art.

- [ ] Use shadows to tell a visual story.

- [ ] Create a fancy decoration you wish existed at the last holiday or themed get-together you attended.

- [ ] Make a piece of art from a family member's favorite flower.

- [ ] Turn your favorite beverage container into the dollhouse you always wanted as a kid.

- [ ] Use one of your best stories (see reflective writing prompts) to create a tiny book, then illustrate the cover.

Create and Curate

- ☐ Depict a place that used to exist but is no longer there.

- ☐ Create a flyer for a fake event that you wish happened in the past.

- ☐ Capture your childhood home in any medium that suits you.

- ☐ Call or message someone you haven't spoken to in years, then paint the emotions you felt when you reconnected.

- ☐ Depict the year 2000 in one scene.

- ☐ Faith, lost then found.

- ☐ Faith, found then lost.

- ☐ Create art around the topic of "first words."

- ☐ Bullies in childhood and bullies now.

- ☐ Depict a fall ritual.

500 Ideas for Artists & Writers

- [ ] Create a totem/cairn that represents scenes from your past.

Create and Curate

- [ ] What if the museum took on a life of its own?

- [ ] Write or depict sacred religious or spiritual traditions.

- [ ] Purge your closets of anything you haven't worn in the past year. Bag everything up and donate it to an organization seeking clothing donations. Write or create art about what this feels like to you.

- [ ] Depict a sacred religious or spiritual tradition.

- [ ] What represents renewal for you visually? Write or illustrate it.

- [ ] You suspect your mail carrier isn't quite who you think they are.

- [ ] What does it feel like to be saved by grace?

- [ ] What is your most dominant emotion today? What is the story behind it? What is the story behind that story?

500 Ideas for Artists & Writers

- [ ] You can never have too much of a good thing?

- [ ] Depict a person looking in a window longingly.

- [ ] Imagine that the objects we use every day did not have names. Spend some time thinking about their use, purpose, and what they look like. Rename them based on your descriptions.

- [ ] What does the science teacher do after leaving school?

- [ ] "They don't make music like that anymore…"

- [ ] The benefits of an empty nest.

- [ ] Moving in with the kids.

- [ ] Create art about an event you missed but wished you had been present for.

- [ ] Write or depict a world in which people no longer die.

Create and Curate

- ☐ Write or create art inspired by your first job.

- ☐ Think about a meal you remember having with family or friends as a child. Capture as many sensory details as you can through art or writing, depicting vivid representations of smells, sounds, textures, visual cues, and, of course, taste.

- ☐ Reflect on the mistakes you have made in life. Turn this situation into a morality story for kids through images.

- ☐ Use your life goals to inspire a piece of art.

- ☐ Create a piece of art based on your favorite thing to do in your spare (HA!) time.

- ☐ Find a current story from the news that either inspires you or evokes a lot of emotion. Create a visual depiction of the story using whatever medium appeals to you.

- ☐ Depict your favorite fairy tale in a modern setting.

500 Ideas for Artists & Writers

- As creators, at times we all have barriers that stand in our way of being creative, such as time and work. Create a piece of art that examines those barriers.

- Create a piece of art based on your favorite meal.

- Create a piece of art based on how you feel just before you fall asleep.

- Driving in an ice storm.

- Standing in a windstorm.

- Memorialize an old technology in an image.

- Illustrate the plot of your favorite book or story.

- Find an old episode of "The Joy of Painting" with Bob Ross, and paint along.

Create and Curate

500 Ideas for Artists & Writers

W

- Write a song or poem about the autumn harvest.

- Write about a character looking back on childhood and having a realization about their parents' true identities.

- A social media influencer who takes things too far.

- The best time to get away with murder is when you're the last person anyone would ever suspect.

- Write a story about someone coming out of hibernation.

- Write a short story about an autumn leaf that hasn't fallen from the tree just yet.

- Write about a misshapen pumpkin and its plight.

Create and Curate

- [ ] Write about a person experiencing the change of seasons for the first time.

- [ ] You are a maple tree afraid of losing your leaves in the fall.

- [ ] Keep a pencil and paper beside your bed. Write down the first thought that comes to mind when you wake up one day and use that as the basis for a story.

- [ ] Write a book review for a book you really didn't enjoy.

- [ ] Visit a cemetery. Pick a headstone and write a story using them as the main character. What was their life like? How did they die?

- [ ] Are kids smarter than adults? If so, how?

- [ ] A holiday spent with strangers.

- [ ] Start listing physical characteristics (height, weight, sad eyes) then list other details (professional golfer, loyal, drinks too much). Keep going until you have a comprehensive

500 Ideas for Artists & Writers

list. Finally, change one major aspect of this character you've created (gender, location, religion, profession). Now write about this person in the midst of their day-to-day life.

- [ ] Describe the city you live in as if it were a person.

- [ ] Write a real estate advertisement for an enchanted house.

- [ ] Write a story about a character in a video game.

- [ ] Your refrigerator has begun a kitchen-wide strike. What happens now?

- [ ] Write a story from the perspective of your television if it were a sentient, omnipotent being.

- [ ] If you were a motorized vehicle, what kind of vehicle would you be and why?

- [ ] Create a scene that shows a busy day at the airport and tell or depict the scene from

Create and Curate

multiple points of view (a passenger, security agent, and a pilot, for instance).

- [ ] Think about three people in your life who are neutral to you—perhaps the neighbor you only see occasionally or the mail person who waves—and write down what you think you know about these people. Now combine the physical characteristics and behaviors you've witnessed to create a new character who must face their greatest fear.

- [ ] Write the story of a person who owns seven identical outfits and despises accessories.

- [ ] Depict a scene in which a person enters a party uninvited.

- [ ] Write a story from the perspective of your shoes.

- [ ] Write a story about a photocopier that became possessed by demons.

- [ ] Start by writing 3-4 character traits about two different characters. Write the dialogue

500 Ideas for Artists & Writers

that occurs between them when they meet for the first time.

- [ ] Choose three people from your social circle (family, colleagues, friends) who do not know each other. Create a story that involves all three of these people meeting each other.

- [ ] Create a character based on your favorite word.

- [ ] The nude art model who didn't get the job.

- [ ] Describe your childhood home in as much detail as possible. Pick one of the spaces in your home that meant something to you and write about why.

- [ ] After so many years of searching, she finally found [insert title], the last book known to exist on earth.

- [ ] Start a story with "What do you mean I can't say that anymore?" or "Kids today…"

Create and Curate

- Write a story about being outside, looking in.

- You are stuck inside a snow globe owned by your nemesis. Write this story using no more than 50 words.

500 Ideas for Artists & Writers

- ☐ You are working from your home office one afternoon when you see a dominatrix enter the house across the street. Write about this neighbor.

- ☐ You are renovating a century-old home and found a box of old photographs tucked behind the plaster and lathe. Describe what you find and what happens next.

- ☐ Write a story about a telephone that can connect to the past.

- ☐ Choose a major historical event you are familiar with. Write a story from the perspective of someone who was a witness to the event.

- ☐ Write a story where the only mode of transportation that exists is on foot.

- ☐ Write a story about a long-lost, undelivered letter.

- ☐ Write a story about making eye contact with someone for the first time.

Create and Curate

- [ ] Write a story about what a memory looks, feels, smells, and tastes like.

- [ ] Use an old, cherished family recipe as the basis for a story.

- [ ] Write a story about regifting something.

- [ ] Choose a story you have previously written and select a paragraph that resonates with you. Rewrite that paragraph two or three more times, using fewer words each iteration. See if you can whittle the paragraph down to less than fifty words but still maintain the intent or meaning.

- [ ] Think of a place that used to exist but is no longer there; somewhere you used to visit. Imagine you are there and write about what you see, feel, hear, smell, and taste.

- [ ] And that was how I met my ...

- [ ] Imagine you were given a "Control Z" moment for your life. Write about a moment in your life where you would either redo or omit altogether. What would have happened differently? How would that have altered the result?

Create and Curate

CONNECT

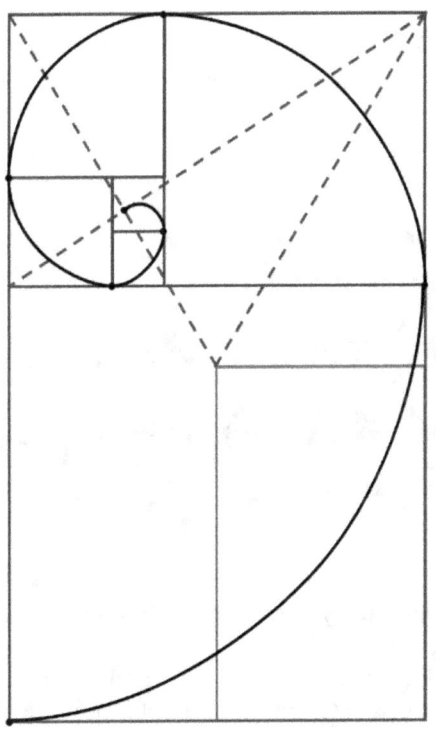

500 Ideas for Artists & Writers

A

- [ ] Depict what happens when one drives beyond this gas station.

- [ ] Two people reconnect at this gas station after ten years. What do they leave behind?

- [ ] Recreate the same image above and add a character or unexpected object to the scene.

Create and Curate

- [ ] An accidental social media influencer who never wanted this life finds a true connection in the 3D world.

- [ ] Juxtapose a childhood pre-internet against a childhood post-internet.

- [ ] Create a piece of art using your non-dominant hand.

- [ ] Create art inspired by holding hands.

- [ ] Sit outside for about an hour. Create a work of art based on the sounds you hear.

- [ ] Create art about the sound of snow.

- [ ] Create a piece of art that depicts the stillness of a winter night.

- [ ] Three sisters remember the same event quite differently.

- [ ] Remember friendship bracelets? Make one for a friend.

500 Ideas for Artists & Writers

- [ ] Going in through the exit door.

- [ ] Draw something with your eyes closed.

- [ ] Create art… in the nude.

- [ ] Reimagine your favorite meal as if it were an outfit.

- [ ] Sidewalk chalk! Now go outside and draw.

- [ ] Reimagine the shadows you see outside your window as objects.

- [ ] Reimagine the people you know as common household objects.

- [ ] Combine two panoramic photos into one image.

- [ ] Paint two different things combined (necklace + flowers, cat + moon, ocean + eyes).

Create and Curate

- ☐ Write or draw about flowers growing in unexpected places.

- ☐ Draw or paint a rainbow animal.

- ☐ Go for a walk and photograph ten random things, then choose one to illustrate.

- ☐ Write a poem or some phrases that would make for good wall art in your home.

- ☐ Try to recreate your first childhood painting (as far as you can remember or imagine).

- ☐ Draw upside down (the paper, but if you are really courageous, hey, go for it!).

- ☐ Think about a song where you have misheard the lyrics. Create art based on the misheard lyrics.

- ☐ Depict an awkward first date.

- ☐ Create art where you have anthropomorphized something familiar, like a floor lamp or car.

500 Ideas for Artists & Writers

- ☐ Create art that includes idioms.

- ☐ Open up a dictionary and pick five words that begin with different letters. Create art that incorporates those five words.

- ☐ One word: Origami!

- ☐ Create art based on the theme of blended families.

- ☐ Mine the internet for images of "What I ordered, versus what I got." Create art based on unmet expectations.

- ☐ Recreate the album cover of your least favorite album for your least favorite band.

- ☐ Create art that revolves around something you cannot live without.

- ☐ Take an afternoon off and go for a swim in your local public pool during public swim hours. Spend some time listening to the sounds underwater. What do you hear? If you have goggles, open your eyes. What do

Create and Curate

you see? How does it feel? Now go create some art!

- [ ] Depict irrelevance or obsolescence.

- [ ] Create art around what achievement or success feels like to you.

- [ ] Create art based on the theme "shoot the messenger."

- [ ] What does it feel like to be keeping a big secret?

- [ ] Create a mixed media project combining different textures.

- [ ] Imagine a visit to a place you've always wanted to go, such as The Museum of Fear and Wonder.

- [ ] Using only colors and geometric shapes, create art that represents the theme of culture shock.

- [ ] Illustrate the ultimate playground.

500 Ideas for Artists & Writers

- [ ] Tell a visual story using doorways.

- [ ] Create whiteboard art.

- [ ] Come up with your own graffiti tag and "sign" something you own.

- [ ] Draw, paint, or construct a character that can be a prompt for writers in our next book.

Create and Curate

W

- Write a short story that begins with the person who left this bike and ends with the person who takes the bike.

- Write from the perspective of a scarecrow who is falling apart.

- If there's a person in your life you can't stand, write a story with this person as your protagonist.

500 Ideas for Artists & Writers

- [ ] Choose a current event that is considered a polarizing issue. Now, rewrite that article from the opposing point of view.

- [ ] Write a letter to a stranger.

- [ ] Using only dialogue, depict a scene where two people are making a gingerbread house.

- [ ] Write a story that includes someone starting their first garden.

- [ ] A character finds an old outfit in the closet that reminds them of the day they last wore it.

- [ ] Write about someone who is the polar opposite of you in every way. What is a day in the life of this person like?

- [ ] What is your greatest fear? Write about a character who has no fear of this person/place/thing.

Create and Curate

- ☐ Write about two characters with polarizing viewpoints meeting in an unexpected way that forces them to connect.

- ☐ A couple falls in love. Who cares about the thirty-year age difference?

- ☐ Write about what love feels like.

- ☐ If you live in or near an urban center, spend some time observing the department store window displays. Create a scene based on the mannequins in the window.

- ☐ Write a story from the perspective of a Christmas tree/snowman.

- ☐ Where does this staircase lead?

500 Ideas for Artists & Writers

- [ ] Write about an activity you are passionate about (reading, running, crafting, etc.) but from the perspective of someone who thinks the opposite of you.

Create and Curate

- [ ] Sit outside on a nice evening after dark. Spend some time stargazing. Create a story where the constellations are characters trying to get home.

- [ ] Disgruntled employees strike and finally demand what they deserve, but the leader is not in a position to give it to them. Write.

- [ ] It's not easy being related to the principal.

- [ ] Depict the dialogue that occurs between winter and spring as the seasons are changing. What do they say to each other?

- [ ] Ask your neighbor about their day or weekend. No matter how boring or vague, write a story about it.

- [ ] Your character: "Finally doing what I love, but it wasn't what I thought it'd be."

- [ ] Imagine your two favorite authors partnered to write a story. What would the title be? Use that title as a catalyst.

500 Ideas for Artists & Writers

- [ ] Write a story that takes place during the crepuscular hours.

- [ ] Write about connections made in the aftermath of a natural disaster.

- [ ] The hospital began turning people away, but the woman on 14th street opened her doors.

- [ ] In this antique shop, everything is negotiable but comes with a story.

- [ ] The cabana began to shake during the storm, but the family found steadiness.

- [ ] The hotel staff is missing, but the missing girl reappeared.

- [ ] The hotel is missing, but the staff was found.

- [ ] Write three poems about the same topic, each one connected to the rhythm of a different song.

Create and Curate

- [ ] Write about the journey of a consumer product, from its origin to its ultimate use.

- [ ] Write a story that spans a single hour of time across three different time zones.

- [ ] Two people meet in a virtual reality bar. Who are they really?

- [ ] Find a short story you really love. Rewrite it as a poem (or vice versa).

- [ ] Write an acrostic poem using the letters of the alphabet in order.

- [ ] Review an old piece of work. Go through it to find out which word is used most often. Remove that word and see what happens.

- [ ] Write ... in the nude.

- [ ] Write an advertisement for a product no one would ever want.

- [ ] Write a story about two people who are lying to each other.

500 Ideas for Artists & Writers

- ☐ Write a story about your readers.

- ☐ What if superpowers were normal, and not having a superpower was considered exceptional?

- ☐ Write a piece inspired by what you can't see.

- ☐ Write about a recent conflict that you dealt with in your life.

- ☐ Write about putting together the pieces of a puzzle.

- ☐ Write a poem or some phrases that would make for good wall art in your bathroom.

- ☐ Write about the moment you discovered your love for what you do.

- ☐ Begin your writing with the phrase "The stage was set."

- ☐ Look out the nearest window. Describe what you see.

Create and Curate

ALCHEMIZE

500 Ideas for Artists & Writers

A

- [ ] Look up an interesting animal fact. Use this fact as a catalyst for creating artwork.

- [ ] A time your character received animal wisdom (think guidance, a warning, a reminder ...).

- [ ] Identify a familiar landmark as a threshold and explore what it symbolizes.

- [ ] Found objects.

- [ ] A plant that grows in an unexpected or unusual place.

- [ ] What lives at the end of the rainbow?

- [ ] Are there more doors in the world, or wheels?

- [ ] Take a walk and collect some objects from nature along the way, such as different

Create and Curate

leaves or pieces of wood. Zoom in on an interesting detail in your objects, such as the veining in a leaf or a knot in a piece of wood, and create art based on this zoomed-in perspective.

- [ ] Do a seasonal craft in a different season (for example, make a wreath in August while drinking hot cocoa).

- [ ] Revisit a piece of art you previously created and don't love. Take scissors to it (you really cannot love this piece) and cut it up into squares. Play around with the squares in different iterations to recreate a new piece of art.

- [ ] Draw or paint your future.

- [ ] Design the cover for your future bestseller.

- [ ] Create your own country: imagine the culture, people, geography, flora, fauna, food, and governance. Go as far as creating a visual depiction of it as well.

500 Ideas for Artists & Writers

- [ ] Instead of using a paintbrush to paint, collect items from nature, such as sticks and grasses to paint with. Experiment by bundling different textures and types together.

- [ ] What does the idiom 'paper tiger' mean to you? Create a piece of art based on this.

- [ ] Begin writing your story by starting at the end.

- [ ] Create a piece of art that depicts growth.

- [ ] Clowns.

- [ ] Running through a field.

- [ ] A time capsule opens.

- [ ] Create a piece of art inspired by the idea of a post-internet world.

- [ ] Depict extreme heat.

Create and Curate

- ☐ What comes to mind when you think about autumn? Write down your thoughts, then create an illustration that captures at least three items from the list.

- ☐ Depict a scene in which one person helps another find warmth.

- ☐ Spiritual experiments with "consciousness-enhancing drugs."

- ☐ Therapy and experiments with cognitive behavioral therapy have gone either really right or really wrong.

- ☐ Raising children and/or not raising children—the power and perils.

- ☐ This teen really does know it all, if only people would listen.

- ☐ We discounted them because they were old, but now we're paying the price.

- ☐ Paint rocks and hide them in your local park.

500 Ideas for Artists & Writers

- [ ] Leave an uplifting message in a place that is normally associated with boredom or waiting.

- [ ] Invite two people who would never ordinarily meet to go to a museum or public art display with you.

- [ ] Plant a tree and dedicate it to your favorite artist or writer.

- [ ] Draw an image that represents the knowledge lost in the burning of the fire of the Library of Alexandria.

- [ ] Create your own black box and illustrate it.

- [ ] Create a new map of the world that represents what you believe it will look like in 100 years, 200 years, or 1,000 years.

- [ ] Visually tell the story of the man who handwashes and line-dries all his clothes, no matter the weather.

Create and Curate

- ☐ If the dogs walked themselves, where would they go?

- ☐ Make a list of everything you did today, then create a piece of art based on that list.

- ☐ Think about what you want to communicate to the people who look at your art. Now communicate that to them in an abstract image.

- ☐ Create a work based on a new moon or full moon ritual.

- ☐ Create a work that depicts the vibrancy of a street fair.

- ☐ Take artistic photos of things you see every day. The more ordinary, the better.

- ☐ Pretend you no longer had access to words. Create a visual language.

- ☐ Create a piece in homage to anyone or anything that has inspired your creativity and artistic passion.

500 Ideas for Artists & Writers

- [ ] Time is frozen in your image.

- [ ] Create art around following in someone's footsteps, either literally or figuratively.

- [ ] A place that was magical to you as a child.

- [ ] Create art around the theme of digital algorithms.

- [ ] Imagine anthropomorphizing your home. What might it be thinking if you were to hold an open house for strangers? Would it be nervous? Wary? Excited? Create art depicting this.

Create and Curate

500 Ideas for Artists & Writers

W

- There were peacocks everywhere.

- Think of a time when you experienced a lot of emotions. Now, imagine those emotions as a type of weather; describe the scene.

- Order Chinese food from your favorite restaurant. Write a story based on the fortune inside your cookie.

- Go through a car wash with your eyes closed. Write what you hear.

- Write a story about what the current world would look like in the absence of the internet.

- Write a story about a road that has no ending and no beginning.

- Write about a person who believes they possess otherworldly powers. No one else

Create and Curate

believes them. Tell the story that reveals who is right.

- ☐ Write about a society where no one feels superior.

- ☐ Depict a scene just before and just after a major natural disaster.

- ☐ A day-in-the-life story from the perspective of your dog or cat or lizard.

- ☐ Describe an object of nature without actually naming it.

- ☐ Think about an animal that thrives in extreme climates. Write about some of the challenges this animal faces living in this environment.

- ☐ Take a photograph of the contents of your recycling bin. Use the image as the inspiration for a story about renewal.

- ☐ Create your own country: imagine what the culture, people, geography, flora, fauna,

500 Ideas for Artists & Writers

food, governance, etc. is like. Go as far as creating a visual depiction of it as well.

- [ ] A spaceship lands in a banker's backyard.

- [ ] Recreate your resume as a short story.

- [ ] Write about a story that never ends.

- [ ] You subscribe to a daily newspaper, which you read front to back every day. Only, the newspaper that was delivered today is actually dated for tomorrow...

- [ ] Write a short story set in the 1980s based on someone who is an influencer today. Write about how this person's life would be different with no social media outlet.

- [ ] You find a camera that takes pictures of the future.

- [ ] Write about a world where seagulls were revered for their greatness, elegance, and beauty.

Create and Curate

- [ ] Write a story where the only method of long-distance communication was via carrier pigeon.

- [ ] It snowed twelve inches overnight ... Only the snow isn't white.

- [ ] What does summer taste like to you?

- [ ] The year is 2245, and dogs have been genetically modified to have intelligence equal to humans.

- [ ] Write three paragraphs, each depicting the unique holiday celebrations of three neighbors.

- [ ] Wardrobe changes—meditate on this.

- [ ] Attend an event you wouldn't ordinarily attend, such as a basketball game or a dance performance. Take note of what happens in the game/performance and use this as the backdrop as you write about a criminal who went to the same performance to hide out.

500 Ideas for Artists & Writers

- [ ] Reread some of your older work, or find an old piece of art. Reinterpret it, starting from scratch.

- [ ] Write a story about a conversation you overheard.

- [ ] Imagine you have a touch of magic and can make impossible things happen. What would you do?

- [ ] Write about waking up.

- [ ] A shoe falls out of the sky. Why?

- [ ] If your brain were a tangible, physical place, what would it be like?

- [ ] Suggest eight possible ways to get a ping pong ball out of a vertical pipe.

- [ ] If I was to follow the pathway to my highest version of myself, what does the string/pathway look like?

Create and Curate

- [ ] A curmudgeon meets an optimist and chaos ensues.

- [ ] Everything was in my mother's purse.

- [ ] Imagine the elements (wind, water, fire, and earth) are people. Who are they? What are they doing?

- [ ] Write your New Year's Resolutions five years in the future.

- [ ] Write about an unseen character.

- [ ] Rewrite an old fairy tale from the perspective of a secondary character.

- [ ] Create a character who does everything they are told. What happens next?

- [ ] Write about stolen identity.

- [ ] If you were to be reincarnated, what would you choose to be?

500 Ideas for Artists & Writers

- [ ] Write in a different space today; if you normally write in your office, choose the bathroom or kitchen today instead.

- [ ] Write about deciding to quit something. And then write about relapsing.

- [ ] Create a story about two characters whose 'love languages' do not align. Perfection? Disaster? You decide.

- [ ] Write a fake news article about an actual news event.

- [ ] Begin a story with someone accepting a bribe.

Create and Curate

500 Ideas for Artists & Writers

Create and Curate

On Inspiration *from the Unleash Team*

500 Ideas for Artists & Writers

Jen Knox

"It's been said in many ways that we look to art to find out what we know or what we think. The process of creativity helps us to examine the world in new ways that can empower, excite, and illuminate the natural beauty of the world as well as the depth of the human imagination. Creative prompts, no matter how silly or strange, have been portals for me that allow new ways of thinking and appreciation of both our world and the possibilities beyond. What could be better than that?"

Create and Curate

The founder and executive director of Unleash Creatives, Jen Knox is an educator and storyteller who teaches writing, leadership, and meditation. Her books include the short story collections *The Glass City* (Hollywood, CA: Winner, Prize Americana for Prose), *After the Gazebo* (New York City, NY: Rain Mountain Press), and *Resolutions: A Family in Stories* (AUXmedia). Her short stories have been featured in textbooks, classrooms, and both online and print publications around the world. Her fiction appears in *The Best Small Fictions 2017 (Braddock Avenue Books), The Adirondack Review, Sivana East, Chicago Tribune's Printers Row, Chicago Quarterly Review, Cosmonauts Avenue, Crannog, Cutthroat Magazine, Juked, McSweeney's Internet Tendency, MJI News, Poor Claudia, The Saturday Evening Post, The Santa Fe Writers Project Quarterly, NPR, Short Story America, and Sequestrum*, among over a hundred other publications.

500 Ideas for Artists & Writers

Ashley Holloway

"Inspiration is both a word and a feeling. As a feeling, it is seductive; it has the capacity to transform how we see ourselves as individuals and how we interact with the world around us. Ever elusive in nature, when we capture it, inspiration is a bit like a drug; it helps us see the world more clearly. Or not. Whatever. You do you. But the best part about this book is simply being inspired by inspiration. Now go be creative and enjoy getting lost in the process."

Create and Curate

Ashley Holloway is a nurse with a potpourri of experience in all aspects of the healthcare system. In addition to her role as faculty in a post-secondary healthcare leadership program in Calgary, AB, Ashley also teaches interdisciplinary teamwork and communication using medical simulation at the Alberta Children's Hospital. Ashley holds a Master of Public Health, as well as a graduate diploma in global leadership, with further studies in intercultural communication and international development. Ashley's work has appeared in the Calgary Public Library Short Story Dispenser, *Flash Fiction Magazine*, *The Nashwaak Review*, *The Globe and Mail*, *Magna Publications*, *The Prairie Journal*, Alberta's *CARE Magazine*, with regular contributions to *Lead Read Today*. Ashley also reads manuscripts and provides editorial support for Unleash Creatives.

500 Ideas for Artists & Writers

Sascha Ealey

"Many of us are visual people. We understand the world through images, shapes, and colors rather than words. Art is made for many purposes and experiencing art is very individual. But whether the purpose is to share beauty or enlighten with ideas or make a statement to capture a moment, place, or person, art always serves to connect the artist with its viewers. Art connects us even across social distances. A connection made over art is not easily lost or forgotten."

Create and Curate

Sascha Ealey was born and raised in Brooklyn, New York, where she still resides with her two children. She decided she wanted to become a writer at the age of seven.

Sascha obtained a bachelor's degree in English at Saint Francis College in Brooklyn Heights. One of her dreams is to use her life experiences to help young women feel understood in a world where society wants them to sweep things under the rug. Her first book, *Dry Bones*, was released in April 2022 by Fulton Books, and she is currently working on her second book as well as a series of short stories. Sascha has been a part of the Unleash team since spring 2022.

500 Ideas for Artists & Writers

Image Attributions

Holloway, Ashley. Unnamed photographs on pages 15, 23, 33, 41, 47, 62, 68, and 76.

Knox, Jen. "Prague" and "Marfa" on pages 52 and 59.

Knox, m.r. "Totem" on page 36.

Shanahan, Christopher J. "Unleash Logo" design on pages IV and 84. Image on 51.

Image on page 8 is "Man Walking on Floor" by Bob Price